Dedicated To:
Estranged families

Written By: Abigail Gartland

Hello, my name is St. Rita!

I was born in Italy in 1381!

I loved Jesus so much ever since I was a little girl.

I wanted to become a sister in a religious order, but my dad thought it was not a good idea.

My family wanted me to get married, and I married a man named Paolo.

We had two boys!

As much as I loved my husband and our two boys, some members of Paolo's family were unkind.

One day, there was a fight with Paolo's family, and my husband died.

On that day, he was called to Heaven to be with Jesus.

I decided to become a sister.

When I arrived at the convent, they said I needed to make sure the family stopped fighting before I could join.

I was so sad, and I did not know what to do to make them stop fighting. I asked Jesus and the saints to help me.

I talked to the family many times, and prayed a lot for them. Eventually, they stopped fighting.

I was able to join the convent and become a sister.

asked Jesus if I could join His suffering. he said yes and gave me a scar on my head to remind me of Him.

Do you want to be more like me?

You can celebrate my feast day with me on May 22nd.

I am the patron saint of hard things!

I pray for your family every day.

St. Rita
Pray for us!

opyright:

part: © PentoolPixie © LimeandKiwiDesigns
ensed purchased: 1/10/2024

About the Author

Abigail Gartland

I love the saints and I love my faith. The idea for sharing the stories of the saints with little ones came when my dear friends were expecting their first baby. I wanted to create something as unique and special as our friendship. Each book is dedicated to very special people and groups who have enriched my faith in different ways. I am blessed to write these stories and appreciate the unending support of my family and friends. When I am not writing, am a middle school teacher. I hope you enjoy these stories. I pray for each and every person who opens one of my books to learn more about the saints.

Abbie

www.ingramcontent.com/pod-product-compliance
Lightning Source LLC
LaVergne TN
LVHW051042070526
838201LV00067B/4893